Ideas
that change
lives

Author:

Sikandar Sami

All progressions are situated in thoughts. Thoughts give us new viewpoints and from those new points of view we're ready to change our practices.

In this little report, I've assembled three thoughts that have impacted my life and which I accept can impact yours.

Thought #1: The Two Minds

Thought #2: How to 80/20 Your Life Idea #3: The Prime Belief

I didn't think of these thoughts myself. On the off chance that you glance around sufficiently hard, you'll see them spring up in a wide range of spots, from business, to NLP, to conventional Self Help, to different types of

treatment.

This is only my interpretation of them and a portion of the manners in which I've applied them. I trust you get something out of them.

Best,

Sikandar Sami

Contents

Thought #1: THE TWO MINDS

Close your eyes. Pause, don't close them yet. Wrap up this passage, at that point close them. Alright, close your eyes and attempt to

consider nothing for 30 seconds. Are you game? Go. (Waiting...)

Wasn't simple right? Odds are different considerations and pictures continued flying into your head.

Presently, I need you to attempt a similar exercise once more, aside from this time I need you to focus on which explicit considerations and pictures spring up. Attempt to monitor them. Notice them,

note what they are, and afterward let them go. Check whether you can do that for a moment.

Are you game? Go. (Waiting...)

What right? Perhaps that battle you had with your sibling a day or two ago. Or on the other hand the task that is expected tomorrow yet you're perusing this. Or on the other hand perhaps a film you saw as of late, or an acceptable version of imagination.

Odds are you had the option to see them for a brief period however then you rapidly wind up getting sucked into pondering them automatically.

In the event that you've at any point contemplated, even a smidgen, you're comfortable with the experience you simply had.

You shut your eyes and attempted to quiet your brain down, regardless of whether for 30 seconds, and notwithstanding your earnest attempts, the nozzle of

thought upchuck simply continued spilling out.

On the off chance that you've at any point gone to reflection withdraws or been associated with some development, for example, Zen like I was for some time, they jabber about this "mind babble" that you endured.

Furthermore, the thing is, that "mind prattle" never stops. It's continually going on in your every day life.

A great deal of these eastern ways of thinking plan to "calm" that

chatterbox of a psyche that we have, and I guess it's helpful to discourage it.

However, I've really found rehearsing such methods have another advantage, an advantage analysts are simply getting on to and beginning to expound on here in the West.

That advantage is the thing that I call the "Two Minds."

At the point when you close your eyes and attempt to take out any contemplations (and flop hopelessly like most of us), clearly your brain is thinking.

In any case, on the off chance that your brain is thinking, at that point who is watching the psyche thinking?

Hold up...

At the point when you did the activity and your brain continued meandering

back to what you needed to accomplish at work tomorrow, who was it that was watching your brain stress over work tomorrow?

It was your psyche watching your brain.

In Zen they allude to this as the "Thinking Mind" and the "Watching Mind." The two personalities.

It's a typical idea in Buddhism and new western

treatments, for example, Acceptance-Commitment Therapy (ACT) are getting on to how helpful it is and how it can illuminate a ton of our regular passionate issues.

I'll separate the Two Minds further and afterward show how

they can be applied to tackling a considerable lot of the passionate issues we manage in our regular daily existences.

The issue with the Thinking Mind is that we don't totally control it.

Try not to trust me? I'll demonstrate it.

Whatever you do, don't consider a pink elephant. Try not to consider a pink elephant holding a blue umbrella with his trunk. Try not to consider a pink elephant once throughout the following

two sections.

Alright, in addition to the fact that you pictured a major pink elephant with a blue umbrella, yet you were watching yourself consider a pink elephant while you were perusing the previous two sections.

Your Observing Mind was watching your Thinking Mind

enjoy pink elephants consistently, notwithstanding the way that it was advising your Thinking Mind not to enjoy said elephants.

The Thinking Mind is continually babbling ceaselessly, while you're holding up in line, while you're sleeping attempting to rest, when you "block out" of discussions with individuals, or when your psyche meanders while perusing (which I'm certain will occur in any event once with me... butt face).

Our Thinking Mind resembles a horny canine on a chain that continues pursuing things and on the off chance that we aren't accustomed to utilizing our

Watching Mind, at that point our Thinking Mind hauls us alongside it.

In the event that our Thinking Mind begins fixating on arriving at level 30 in Diablo or the last scene of Mad Men, our Observing Mind is defenseless to reign it in.

The equivalent goes for feelings. Furthermore, that is really where the vast majority of our experiencing comes – not from the negative feelings

themselves, however from the way that we're defenseless from getting sucked into the negative feelings.

A large portion of our mental and enthusiastic pressure happens in light of the fact that our Thinking Mind and Observing Mind are "melded" and we don't perceive the distinction.

Individuals ask me constantly, "How would I quit feeling so envious?" or "How would I quit feeling so irate?" or "How would I not get apprehensive in this circumstance any longer?"

The appropriate response is you don't. You can't control your Thinking Mind. Those feelings spring up and will keep on springing up.

Try to not combine with those feelings when they emerge.

In Zen, they instruct that rather concerning saying, "I am furious," to state, "I feel outrage." Instead of saying, "I am anxious," state, "I feel apprehension." Instead of saying, "I am envious," you state, "I feel envy."

It might appear to be an unpretentious contrast, yet attempt it. Think about a period as of late when you felt a negative feeling, a great deal of outrage or apprehension or uncertainty.

Presently, rather than intuition, "I resented my sibling," think rather, "I felt outrage towards my sibling." You HAD outrage, however you weren't constrained by the indignation.

Feelings are not a decision. Conduct is.

Individuals ask me constantly, "How would you manage fearing disappointment?" or "How would you not stress over being dismissed?"

I manage dread and stress by managing trepidation and stress. (I know, that is a truly irritating answer.)

I feel a similar dread and stress any other individual does; I simply don't relate to it. I acknowledge it and proceed onward notwithstanding it.

I don't let my Thinking Mind control me. I defuse from my feelings. At the point when I feel dread, I deliberately decide to act regardless of it. At the point when I feel stress, I intentionally decide to act regardless of it.

For example, when I need to plunk down and compose a ton (like composing this PDF), I frequently get apprehensive. I need to compose

something truly extraordinary on the grounds that I know a great many individuals are going to understand it.

One consequence of this apprehension is lingering.

At the point when I was more youthful and I was in circumstances where I got apprehensive and procrastinated (i.e., a major research paper in school), I would conclude, "I can't do it since I'm excessively drained," or "I can't center like others, I should have ADD or something."

This was me being melded with my Thinking Mind. There was no partition between my feelings and my personality.

I felt apprehensive and had an idea of "I can't do it for X, Y or Z reason," and I acknowledged it at face esteem. I was a captive to my Thinking Mind, pulled by its chain.

Nowadays I'm frequently ready to plunk down and compose 5,000 words or more in a solitary day. I despite everything feel a similar tension. I despite everything hear similar contemplations ("I have to eat first," "I should sleep," "I'm not in a composing mind-set at the present time.")

In any case, presently as opposed to relating to these contemplations, I recognize them:

"I feel apprehension about composing today." "I have the idea that I have to eat first."

"I have the idea that I have to sleep first."

And afterward I go to my Thinking Mind and quickly disclose to him that it's brimming with crap and that I needn't bother with a damn thing but to sit my butt down and begin composing.

We as a whole produce reasons and negative feelings automatically.

Prepare to be blown away. That is NEVER going to change.

I couldn't care less what number of positive musings you invoke, what sort of treatments you do, or what sort of New Agey otherworldly

poop you think of – negative considerations and feelings are common cycles of the human mind.

You can't escape from them. None of us can.

What you CAN do is acknowledge them. Defuse from them. And afterward act in spite of them.

At the point when individuals arrive at me request that how "Quit feeling furious," or "Quit getting apprehensive," this is their concern. When you attempt to dispense with an idea or feeling, you make it more grounded.

The more you center around a feeling, the more impressive it becomes.

Negative feelings resemble sand trap, the more you battle to escape them, the further into them you sink.

Try to acknowledge them and afterward let go. This is an ability and it is a cycle, yet it can't be polished until you perceive that there are two personalities and you just control one of them.

Here are a few activities you can do that will assist you with isolating your two personalities and in this manner assume greater responsibility for your practices notwithstanding your musings and feelings.

1.   Whenever you feel a compelling feeling or thought, disidentify with it and afterward claim it.

"My manager isn't a dolt. In any case, I am having the idea that my supervisor is an imbecile."

"I don't loathe my ex. I am feeling scorn toward my ex."

"I am not desolate and discouraged. I am feeling dejection and sadness."

Language is extremely amazing. Notice when you disidentify from these feelings and contemplations thusly it: 1)

suggests that they're transitory states, and not perpetual conditions and 2) drives you to assume liability for

them. They're no one's shortcoming, they simply are.

2.   Thank your Thinking Mind for negative contemplations and feelings. This is a strategy from ACT and it is successful. It might sound totally nuts, however it's compelling in light of the fact that it FORCES you to acknowledge your negative feelings rather than battle them.

"Much obliged to you Thinking Mind for feeling apprehensive before my date today. It will cause me to remain alert!"

"Much obliged to you Thinking Mind for being angry at my chief. I truly acknowledge the amount you give it a second thought."

This is going to feel truly odd — offering thanks towards negative feelings. In any case, I think you'll see that it reduces the intensity of the considerations and feelings after some time and really instigates you to make a move regardless of them.

3.   Finally, in the event that you end up seemingly out of the blue, or if there's something that is truly bothering at you, give this a shot.

Take something that is irritated you as of late and hold it in your psyche. Perhaps it's your better half annoying you.

Perhaps it's being unnerved of conversing with that charming young lady in class close to you. Possibly it's leaving your place of employment.

Distil it into a solitary sentence, for example, "I feel scared of leaving my place of employment." Or "I feel aggravated with my sweetheart."

Presently close your eyes and envision Bugs Bunny saying it, while biting a carrot. At that point Mickey Mouse saying it,

while moving and doing cartwheels. Imagine the Chipmunks are singing it to you as a Christmas ditty.

Presently, transform it into a picture, perhaps your irate sweetheart, or your broke ass sitting on the check. Put that picture on a TV screen. Make the hues amusing, give yourself a spotted suit. Make your better half's hair into a

pack of treats sticks.

Make the idea look and sound totally ludicrous in your psyche. Take as much time as is needed and play with it. Attempt to make yourself giggle.

After you've done this for a moment or two, stop. How would you feel?

Odds are you feel greatly improved about it and the negative feeling isn't close to as strong as it was previously.

Isolating your Observing Mind from your Thinking Mind is a propensity that takes practice. In any case, when you start to do it, you'll feel yourself getting less and to a lesser extent a captive to your considerations and your feelings. You'll assume greater responsibility for your inside every day

life and rest easy thinking about it.

As I would like to think, this is simply the absolute most significant advance to creating self-control and acting regardless of whatever depressions or mental hang ups you may experience the ill effects of.

When you've separated your two personalities, you can start to assess your considerations and sentiments from a target put and choose which ones are useful and which ones are harmful (which is something we'll get to in Idea #3).

Thought #2: HOW TO 80/20 YOUR LIFE

In 1906 there was an Italian business analyst named Vilfredo Pareto. One day Pareto saw that consistently 20% of the pea pods in his nursery created around 80% of the peas.

This made him consider monetary yield for a bigger scope. Sufficiently sure, he started to find that in different businesses,

social orders and even organizations, 80% of the creation frequently originated from the 20% most profitable group.

This got known as the Pareto Principle, or what is currently regularly alluded to as the 80/20 Principle.

The 80/20 Principle expresses that 80% of the yield or results will originate from 20% of the information or activity.

The 80/20 Principle has truly been generally mainstream in business the board circumstances.

Organizations regularly found that generally 20% of their clients got 80% of their deals. They found that about 20% of their agents brought 80% of the deals to a close. They found that 20% of your costs lead to 80% of their costs.

As far as time the executives, they frequently found that 20% of their time made 80% of their efficiency, and that 20% of their representatives made 80% of the worth.

The models continue endlessly. Also, obviously, no one was really there with a measuring stick allotting precisely 80% and 20% for these things, however the inexact 4-TO-1 proportion

sprung up continually. Regardless of whether it was really 76/24 or 83/17 is insignificant.

The 80/20 Principle turned into a famous administration device that was utilized generally to expand proficiency and viability inside organizations and businesses.

It's still broadly educated today.

In any case, hardly any individuals thought to apply the 80/20 Principle to regular daily existence or the implications it could have.

For example:

- What are the 20% of your assets you get the most incentive out of?

- What do you invest 20% of your energy doing that gives you 80% of your joy?

- Who are the 20% of individuals you're near who make you the most joyful?

- What are the 20% of the garments you wear 80% of the time?

- What's the 20% of food you eat 80% of the time?

Odds are these are simple inquiries for you to reply. You've quite recently never thought about them.

What's more, when you've addressed them, you can undoubtedly concentrate on

expanding the efficiencies throughout your life. For example, the 80% of individuals you invest energy with who just include 20% of the joy in your life (invest less time with them). The 80% of poo you utilize 20% of the time (toss it out, sell it). The 80% of the

garments you wear 20% of the time (same thing).

Distinguishing the 20% of the food you eat 80% of the time will likely clarify whether you keep a solid eating routine or not and how sound it is. Hello, who needs to follow an eating regimen? Simply do sure to change to where the 20% of food you eat 80% of the

time is sound.

At the point when I initially thought about how the 80/20 Principle applied to my own life, I right away understood a couple of things.

1.   A not many of my interests (TV programs and computer games) represented 80% of my time just brought me 20% of my satisfaction.

2.   A not many of my companions who I invested 80% of my energy with I didn't generally appreciate being near (subsequently I was unsettled in my public activity).

3.   80% of what I spent my cash on was not valuable or solid for my way of life.

Perceiving these things inevitably enlivened some heavy

changes in my decisions and my way of life. I dropped computer games and TV for one. I put forth attempts to recognize different companions

to invest more energy with, and I gave more consideration to what I purchased with my cash.

Also, obviously, the 80/20 Principle can at present be applied to efficiency at work.

What errands do you invest 80% of the energy doing that get 20% of the profits (i.e., browsing email again and again, composing notices, setting aside a long effort to make essential and irrelevant

choices, and so on.)?

What is the 20% of your work that gets you 80% of the credit and acknowledgment from your group or chief?

Lastly, you can apply the 80/20 Principle to your passionate life and connections too. What are the 20% of practices that cause 80% of the issues in your

connections? What are 20% of the discussions that make 80% of the closeness with your accomplice?

These are significant inquiries that the greater part of us never at any point consider.

It doesn't happen to us that there's a proficiency to each part of our life, to all that we do. What's more, not exclusively is there a productivity, however we have a control and impact over that effectiveness, it's something we can assume liability for and

improve.

What changes would you be able to make in your life today dependent on the 80/20 Principle?

It's not really an inflexible guideline for effective living, however consider it a device, a focal point to see parts of your life through.

Plunk down and consider it, possibly work it out. You'll probably be astonished the acknowledge you come to.

.

Thought # 3: THE PRIME BELIEF

In the MID-19TH century, a kid was naturally introduced to a rich family. From the earliest starting point, the kid endured genuine medical problems: an eye issue that left him briefly blinded as a kid, a

horrendous stomach condition that constrained him onto a severe eating routine, and back agonies that would torment him for an incredible duration.

Notwithstanding his dad's objection, he sought to turn into a painter when he grew up. He rehearsed his specialty however for quite a long time and years, each endeavor finished in disappointment. In the interim, his

sibling proceeded to turn into a widely acclaimed author. As he entered adulthood, a large number of his medical issues exacerbated, his relationship with his dad self-destructed, and the youngster

started to battle with extreme episodes of gloom and self-destructive contemplations.

Urgent to fix his child's circumstance, the youngster's dad utilized his business associations with get the youngster admitted to Harvard Medical School. Luckily, the youngster was brilliant. He could deal with the coursework. However, he never felt comfortable or settled at Harvard. In the wake of visiting a mental office one day, the youngster considered in his journal that he believed he shared more practically speaking with the patients than the other

specialists.

Disappointed with his clinical preparing, the youngster searched for different open doors inside foundation that may have fit him. He was frantic. He was eager to take a stab at anything, in any event, something radical and totally extraordinary.

He before long found an anthropological undertaking to the Amazon rainforest. The youngster marked on, eager to get

away and start once more, to maybe find something new and fascinating about the world and about himself.

Back then, intercontinental travel was for some time, confounded and perilous. Yet, the youngster made it to the Amazon. There he speedily contracted smallpox and almost kicked the bucket alone in the wilderness. He was surged back to development and the campaign abandoned him. After recuperating from smallpox, his back fits returned more awful than at any other time. He was starved from the ailment, stuck in an unfamiliar land alone with no real way to impart, and kept on existing in an every day unbearable agony.

The youngster figured out how to get back to a baffled dad, almost 30 years of age, still jobless, a disappointment at all that he had ever endeavored, with a body that double-crossed him and wasn't probably going to ever improve. In spite of each bit of leeway and opportunity he had been given throughout everyday life, he had bombed them all. The main constants throughout his life appeared to be

enduring and disillusionment. The man fell into a profound wretchedness and intended to end his own life.

Above all, he had a thought.

He settled on a concurrence with himself. In his journal, he composed that he would attempt a trial. He would burn through one whole year accepting that he was 100% liable for everything

that happened in his life, regardless. During this period, he would give it his best shot to change his conditions, regardless of the result. On the off chance that, he composed, toward the finish of one year of

assuming liability for everything in his life and attempting to improve it, in the event that nothing in his life had really improved in that time, at that point it will be obvious that he was genuinely weak to

the conditions around him. And afterward he would end his own life.

The youngster's name was William James, the dad of American brain science and one of the most compelling logicians of the previous 100 years. Obviously, he wasn't these things yet, however he would proceed to become them in huge part because of his test. James would later allude to his trial as his "resurrection," and would acknowledge it for all that he would later achieve.

There is an acknowledgment from which all potential

self-improvement develops. This is the acknowledgment that you are liable for all that you do in your life, regardless of the outside conditions.

In 1879, fifteen years in the wake of making the arrangement with himself, William James gave what was maybe his most renowned talk, named "The Will to Believe."

In it, he contended that whether strict or nonbeliever, entrepreneur or

socialist, everybody is compelled to receive values on some level of confidence. Regardless of whether you don't trust in confidence, that is itself a worth

requiring confidence. He proceeded to state that on the off chance that we as a whole should esteem

something, at that point we should situate ourselves to esteem what is generally advantageous for us and others.

At the point when we become liable for our own qualities, we no longer need to battle to cause the world to adjust to our necessities,

Or maybe we can adjust our own qualities to fit the conditions that stand up to us on the planet.

It's that straightforward decision to assume liability for ourselves and our own qualities that permits us to feel in charge of everything

that happens to us and permits us to change our negative encounters into engaging encounters. It's totally

strange, the possibility that being liable for the entirety of the appalling mishaps that happen to us could some way or another free us from them, however it's actual. Our duty regarding ourselves releases a more profound satisfaction by permitting us to interpret

Boisterous children award us the chance to be a decent parent and impart order and duty. A cutback at work awards us the chance to explore different avenues regarding new vocation ways we had consistently wandered off in fantasy land about. A horrendous separation gives us the

opportunity to investigate ourselves and how our practices influence our associations with friends and family.

Truly, these encounters despite everything hurt like a mother lover. Be that as it may, negative encounters are essential forever. The inquiry isn't whether we have them however what we do with them.

Duty permits us to use our agony for strengthening, to change our enduring into quality, our misfortune into circumstance.

James wasn't moronic however. He realized that qualities require in excess of a basic decision to trust them. You don't simply wake up one day and choose, "I'm a glad effective individual!" and

become it. Qualities must be developed, intentionally attempted and

tried and prepared by understanding. Qualities are useless in the event that they don't contain a type of certifiable sign, a few

substantial advantage as certain experience.

We don't generally control what befalls us. Be that as it may, we generally

control a) how we decipher what befalls us, and b) how we react to what exactly transpires. Accordingly, regardless of whether we

intentionally remember it or not, we are consistently liable for

our encounters. Deciding to not intentionally decipher occasions in our lives is as yet an understanding of the occasions of our lives.

Deciding to not react to the occasions in our lives is as yet a reaction to the occasions of our lives.

Regardless, we are continually playing a functioning job

in what is happening with ourselves. We are continually deciphering the importance of each second and each event. We are continually making qualities for ourselves as well as other people. Furthermore, we are continually picking our activities dependent on those qualities. Continuously.

Regardless of whether we understand it or not, we are now picking our activities. We are as of now liable for our negative encounters. We simply aren't generally aware of it.